SEASONS

A MEMOIR BY
DEANA ADKINSON

Copyright @2023 by Deana Adkinson Millin

Seasons

By Deana Adkinson Millin

Printed in the United States

All rights reserved solely by the author. The author guarantees all contents are original and do not infringe upon the legal rights of any other persons or work. No part of this book may be reproduced in any form without the permission of the author. The views are not necessarily those of the publisher.

ACKNOWLEDGMENTS

Writing this book has been one of the biggest accomplishments, yet biggest hurdles of my life. I had to relive every emotion all over again. I would often stop and find myself taking breaks, which turned into a month and then six. Yet I was determined. I would first like to thank God for giving me the courage, strength, motivation, and vision for my first book. I pat myself on the back for pushing through. I can say today I am proud of me! But I cannot not acknowledge those that helped me get here. First and foremost, my book coach and publisher, Coach Dana Watson. Your patience and understanding are unmatched. You have given me opportunity after opportunity to tell my story with the hopes of encouraging someone else. I am forever indebted. My husband, the love of my life, for loving me anyway. For being my backbone and my comfort when it got a little too tough. Thank you for seeing me, baby! My mother, my mama because, without you, your guidance, patience, love, and understanding, I wouldn't be the woman I am today. My children, my three Jays, for allowing me to be the vessel, and for loving me no matter what. For forgiveness and unconditional love. My brother, Big Bro, you did an amazing job, please know that. It was not your burden to carry, and I love you for trying to keep me as pure as possible. Your sacrifices are not unnoticed. My best friends for loving me through it all, with me and for me. My family, for your support and unconditional love. And to all the villains that helped turn my pain into a tool and my trauma into power! I forgive you. And I thank God for your portion. Good or bad!

Blessings to all.

TABLE OF CONTENTS

Introduction 7
Part One: Summer... 9
Part Two: Autumn 29
Part Three: Winter... 43
Part Four: Spring 87
Conclusion 105

"No one's life is a smooth sail; we all come into stormy weather. But it's this adversity, and more specifically, our resilience that makes us strong and successful."
Tony Robbins

INTRODUCTION

We all have seasons in our lives, just like the weather. Some seasons last longer than others. Some winters are colder, summers hotter, nonetheless, we all have them, and our higher power brings us through them. What matters most is that we mature in each season and learn the life lessons as they unfold. I, Deana Adkinson Millin, would like to elaborate on the seasons of my life.

PART ONE

SUMMER

"In summer, the song sings itself."
— William Carlos Williams

I like to think of my childhood as the summer of my life. When life was carefree and fun. Born to a remarkable and extraordinary woman, I am her second child. The only girl with one older brother by four years. Of course, I have a father (as we all do), but he abandoned my mother for a woman he met when my mama was nine months pregnant with me.

You see, at the time, I didn't know I came from strength. My mama is the pure definition of just that. She loved that man with all she knew but he didn't love her the same.

My parents started dating while Mama was still in high school. We will call my father… Drummer Boy. He was in college. Mom moved to DC with her cousin, got pregnant with my brother, and then moved back home. Mama and Drummer Boy decided to give their love another try. At the time, Drummer Boy stood up like a man should and began to raise my brother as his own.

Things began to go south for them before I was born. They planned for me, but things didn't work out for them—Mama was left heartbroken and devastated. Drummer Boy was a rolling stone. He was a "drummer" and singer in a local band. Living the band life back then was, of course, similar, if not the same, as dating a rapper today. Drugs and females. Mama picked up the pieces quickly though and began to raise my brother and I on her own.

For the foundation of my childhood, I would describe it as a small thunderstorm, but for Mama, I'm sure it felt more like a Hurricane. I did spend time with Drummer Boy on occasions, but I saw that red and white child support label in the mailbox more than I can remember times with him.

One weekend in particular, I was with Drummer Boy and his family. He allowed his wife (not the woman he left Mama for) to cut off my natural, long, coarse hair and put a jerry curl in it. She was definitely being asinine and picking with Mama. Mama was livid. If my grandma wasn't there to grab Mama, it may have been a murder scene. She was trying to mock my mother who had a jerry curl herself. Back then, it was the style.

Needless to say, that was the last time I remember spending with my father. Mama did what she should have (I'm a parent, I get it now)—put boundaries on his visitation. Drummer Boy didn't like being told what to do. As an only child, he was used to doing what he wanted and, you guessed it, when he wanted. He didn't appreciate the rules, so he stopped playing all together.

I had what I thought was a normal childhood. Playing outside was not a big deal for me. I feared everything. If it wasn't human, I was afraid. Birds, flies, ants, worms… you name it. Even leaves. Around four or five years old, Mama experienced a financial thunderstorm.

Mama and I moved in with her friend, my Godmother and my God-sister while Big Bro lived with Granny. A rain cloud formed, and I began to feel and display anger at about age eight, which is when I started to ask about my father's whereabouts.

I was a girl scout at the community center. We had a father/daughter dance. This is the first time I remember feeling left out. Feeling different. I felt left out because I was the only girl scout that didn't have an active father in her life.

By the time I saw my father again, I was around 11. For whatever reason (because I look just like a mix between his parents), paternity needed to be established. I saw him that day and not again until after high school.

I wouldn't see him again until I was a young adult. A friend of mine graduated from college. When the ceremony is over, most family and friends gather outside of the building in anticipation of congratulating and loving on their loved one. Once I hugged my friend, I saw a familiar guy not too far from where I was standing.

I just knew that I knew him. Then I said out loud to myself, that's my dad.

I walked over to him and tapped him on his shoulder. He turned around with a look of confusion on his face. He was there to support his stepdaughter who he had raised as his own.

I said, "Excuse me, sir, I know you."

He still had the dumb look of confusion.

I then said, "I'm your daughter, Deana."

His mouth dropped. He said, "Oh my goodness, it is you."

I gave him my number, but that was pointless as he never called.

He wasn't there to teach me my worth, my purpose, or how a man is supposed to treat a woman. And I was mad as hell about it. I didn't know what to do with anger at that age other than to stuff it. Sound familiar?

I was a tomboy, especially with having an older brother around. We were close growing up.

He was and still is my protector. When I was about nine years old, I was outside playing with my friends on a hot summer day. Back then, there wasn't no running in and out of the house. If you came inside too many times, you had to stay in and miss out on all the fun. Don't get too thirsty, and God knows, you better hold your pee.

A group of guys—some so-called friends of my big brother—were among the group. One of the guys offered me some soda… Sprite to be exact. Again, I was young, naive, and extremely gullible. A free soda? Heck yeah, let me get that.

One of the guys called himself being generous and told me to drink it. It was actually urine. A friend of Big Bro was there, so that pissed Big Bro off. He ended up fighting his friend to protect his little sister. That's my first memory of his protection, but I could write a separate book about how much he has protected me. Big Bro was my umbrella when the clouds began to pour. At this point, the rainstorm, Big Bro, countless cousins, and friends could not fill the void I felt.

Soon after, the sun began to shine a little and Mama, Big Bro, and I moved back into a place of our own, in an active community with lots of kids. I met a girl walking to school one morning.

Her mom called me over and asked me if her daughter could walk to school with me. I said yes. We became best friends and, eventually, more like sisters. She had lots of brothers and sisters—over five. So, that made activities and playing at her house more fun than being at mine.

We were inseparable. If you saw her, you saw me, and vice versa. During the school year, I usually spent every weekend at her house, and in the summer, I forgot what my house looked like.

Her parents were popular. All the kids loved her mama. She was fun. Weekends were lit. Her mama would play loud music, allow other kids to come over, and we would party or turn up on music, candy, Kool-Aid, and each other.

For the most part, those times were great, but you know there's no summer without a little rain. Always a calm before the storm, they say.

My friend's mama was extremely generous—a heart of gold. If you were hungry, she would feed you. If you needed clothes, she would give you the shirt off her back. A place to stay… there were no extra beds, but you could get the couch.

Two older brothers needed her help. She was everybody's ma! Ma let them stay with them and looked at and treated them like sons. The brothers would watch us younger kids when she wanted to party. Because my friend and I were the oldest, we got the extra privileges… thirds on dinner and drinks, extra snacks, staying up later than the other kids. We soon became their "girlfriends" when their real girlfriends were not around.

It started with little kisses, then dry humping, to eventually full-blown forced oral on them and each other to sodomy. At that age, I didn't think anything was wrong with what they were doing to us.

I kind of liked the male attention and didn't know or understand that it was the wrong kind of attention. The sodomy was painful and extremely uncomfortable at first, but the attention outweighed the pain, and the pain eventually went away.

This happened often. I didn't tell and I don't know why. I didn't understand that this was wrong until I was about 14. I felt like it was my fault for somewhat liking the attention. I just tried to forget about it.

Mama didn't have a whole bunch of kids in and out of her house, but Big Bro and I were allowed to have occasional sleepovers. It became hard to forget about the brothers when one of Big Bro's friends would play "girlfriend" with me too! He didn't go as far, but touching and feeling and making me do the same was enough.

Ok, so it's pouring now… I didn't know how to process what had happened to me. Or how I was supposed to feel.

I have a close family, we would often get together for cookouts, of course, holidays, and sometimes just because. My family, like most black families, have traditions. One of ours was to pick with the children.

One of my uncles would make my cousin and I fight each other. I hated it. My family didn't know what I had been through, so they didn't realize that teasing and picking was the exact opposite of what I needed.

By now, my friend had moved away and we somewhat grew apart. I had other friends that I was extremely close with in middle school, into my freshman year in high school. I had my family and two close friends.

One friend was like a sister to me too. We were close—our mothers were very close too. This friend's mom was very sick though. We were in 8th grade. My mama and her father were in the school office, and we were called for early dismissal. My friend's mama had passed away.

I had experienced death before, but I never felt pain like that. It was as if my own mama had passed away. She was the mama that understood me—she was me. We are both Aries and she discovered my singing voice!

I was so hurt and felt the all-too-familiar feeling of abandonment yet again. First, Daddy, and now my friend's mama!

Because my friend's mama passed away, she moved in with her dad. We talked sometimes but we were not as close as we once were.

So, I became closer to my two homies. We were our own little version of TLC. We all had our own personalities, but we got each other.

We loved each other. Even got in trouble together.

We were gonna be the freshest in our "friendship pics" in our POLO shirts and jeans… the only problem was we didn't have the money to pay for it, so... yep, you guessed it, we stole the shirts and... yep, you guessed it again, we got caught!

First run-in with the law!

Me and my two homies got into big trouble. I was on punishment for a long time. I had to go straight to school and back home. Mama did allow me to continue to cheer as it was school-related.

Homie #1 got in trouble too and her punishment was lenient. Not so much the same for Homie #2. Her stepfather was very strict, so her punishment was the worst.

She was removed from the squad and was on punishment for so long, her parents forgot she was on it. We would sneak to her house before and after practice to see her. My homies loved me for me, and they got Deana, but that pain and anger was still there. Because... it was still raining.

Being teased by not only family but schoolmates left me angry with an extremely low self-esteem. I was not as developed as my classmates. This caused me to become very self-deprecating.

One day in 8th grade, I was in the bathroom and one classmate thought it would be funny to make a joke out of me by attempting to put tissue in my little training bra. The bathroom was full of girls all laughing, joking, and pointing at me—I was devastated. That devastation brewed more anger.

That anger turned into a tornado.

By 9th grade, I had an 'Idgaf' attitude. I was sad and angry but tried to play class clown to mask it.

I was a cheerleader in 9th and 10th grade. We had a tight squad. I was proud to be on the squad and felt a sense of sisterhood.

My two homies were on the squad too and I had also become close with a new friend who would eventually become my bestie!

I had hella kick it for these chicks. We spent a lot of time together. One of the homies had an older brother, but he was a lot older than her, so her mother would take all of us on vacations, to theme parks, carnivals, girls' days out… all of the fun!

Homie #1 would have the biggest and best sleepovers too.

We went to Kings Dominion one early spring. I remember feeling out of place. I was the fifth wheel that day as my two homies were allowed to bring their boyfriends along. I didn't have one at the time.

I got into a fistfight later that night with Homie #1's boyfriend. He was also my friend—my male best friend. We had known each other the longest.

Our "friendship" would develop into something, but that comes later in the book. So, for now and in this part of the book, we were like brother and sister, and everyone thought we were like God-bro and God-sis at school.

We got into an argument; I don't remember why. Thinking back, I would say jealousy as I had a crush on him since the 4th grade when we met, and I was trying to respect my homie's relationship. More about him later.

I wasn't tight with everyone on the team, except my two homies and Bestie and maybe two other girls. I definitely wasn't one of the coach's favorites, but the sun was starting to shine again for me.

Until one day, I was humiliated all over again in front of the whole squad by the coach.

Born 4 pounds 6 oz., about 19 inches long, I have ALWAYS been petite. But when she called me Olive Oil, it crushed my spirit!

She was one of the adults in my life that I was afraid of and I didn't want to get kicked off the squad, so I didn't say anything! And because I didn't say anything, it made her comfortable enough to call me Olive Oil again and again.

And I just ate it.

She had her picks and her favorites, and I think we all knew and felt that.

Even to this day, I never received recognition as if she expected me to fail or be "A statistic". One comment on social media recently, which came as a surprise.

I wish she would have poured into me back then. And I wish she would have known the damage her innocent jokes would cause!

I was cool but not close with a couple of different chicks. By being a cheerleader, it came with a little clout. So, from time to time, I would hang out with other girls. Me and this one chick hit it off because our attitudes were similar, and we were crushing on a set of brothers. We also had a small crush on two upper classmen.

Mama worked late, which gave me lots of opportunity to be sneaky. Me and Role Dog decided to invite them over after school one day. Role Dog and her guy were in one room and me and my guy in mine.

I had lost my virginity the prior summer but wasn't comfortable getting down with someone else, so I respectfully declined his advances. He wasn't too happy about that.

When we got back to school that Monday, he started a rumor, and by Friday, I found myself in the middle of a hurricane.

Everyone thought I had given him oral. I was not interested in oral sex.

My older cousin told me over and over that if I ever gave someone some head, I would die. And I believed him!

Then there's Bestie. We had been friends since 7th grade but became tight in 9th.

She and I were two peas in a pod. We still are. She's the first girl I said forget it and went against all rules with. Amongst other things.

We skipped school often with the football and basketball players to smoke and chill. We would party but held each other accountable most of the time.

Our backgrounds were not the same. We clicked because of our love for music. We just clicked. They say you get one great friend in a lifetime, and she's my girl.

After a big football game, homecoming to be exact, we went to a house party and stayed later than the rest of the guests because we were those girls that were cool with the guys. Mainly because we were down to earth but mostly because we wanted to smoke up their weed.

Against my better judgment and after the first rumor, I had become promiscuous and slept with one of the football players. I got to school on Monday and once again found myself in the clouds. He ran with the first rumor and accused me of the same thing. I wasn't hurt this time... more like pissed off because, yeah, I had slept with him, but I still wasn't into the oral thing. This just added more fuel to that angry fire burning in my soul.

It was eventually just me and Bestie. My two homies had become closer to other friends, and after we got caught stealing, it wasn't the same. Same love but we kind of started growing apart. I started getting into things they just weren't into.

Plus, we were into smoking and my two homies were not. Homie #1, a male friend and I had tried it the first time together. And I tried it again with one of my other friends that was also a cheerleader, but we didn't make it a habit.

Bestie and I were a totally different story.

I could talk about our high times for hours, but I'll give you this story...

Big Bro bought me my first car.

Instead of being concerned with driving, I would get rides or catch the bus. We lived across the street from the bus terminal, so getting around was not an issue at the time.

The main reason I was not interested in driving was because the car Big Bro got me was a stick. I got frustrated real fast and that frustration would turn into anger, so I used the car as my personal hot box.

Bestie and I would sit in the car and smoke.

We smoked so much one night, we laughed until tears rolled down our eyes. We stopped for a few minutes but couldn't even remember what we were laughing about, which made us laugh again. It felt like 30 minutes but was probably more like 10.

I had a car, and the bus stop was right across the street, but when it was warm out, Bestie and I would walk wherever we wanted to go. We had the nickname footing it asses because we would never let not having a ride stop us from getting to where we wanted to be.

We were a wild pair.

One night, we were chilling with two male friends in Virginia Beach. One friend's parents were gone for the weekend, so we went there to party. Of course, they wanted us to have sex with them, but we decided to make them pay to watch us.

We were two lustful teens curious about how it would feel to willingly touch another woman and performed oral sex on each other. She was the first female I had sex with that I wanted to. Being a child and forced to do it was totally different than wanting to.

So, back to Bro. Like I said, we met in 4th grade and he lived in the same apartment complex as me. On the first day of school, he introduced himself and we became cool after that. We rode the same bus and played with the same group of friends after school and on the weekends. Went to middle and high school together and were hella close. In fact, we were so close, I was the only friend allowed in his house when his mom was not home. Or when she was sleeping.

She worked nights and slept during the day. She didn't like people to knock on the door and wake her up and would yell and say, "Who is that?" He would say, "Deana," and she would be like, "Oh," and get back to resting.

He would eventually drop out of school, but we remained close. One day, we were chilling in his room, smoking and listening to music. We made the wrong decision to overstep our friendship boundaries. We started having sex at the end of my 11th-grade year.

By the way, let me add that he and Homie #1 were long done and over with! Yeah, I know, it didn't make it right, but I never said I wouldn't be the villain in someone else's story.

He was a bit of a player and a typical teenage boy with hormones. We were having sex behind closed doors, but to the world, we were just tight like that. You know… "brother and sister".

After what I had been through with the molestation and the rumors, I hid the feelings that had developed for him after numerous rejections and excuses to why we couldn't be a couple but could creep.

I told myself I was content with the sex. Even if I truly wanted more. I was content with feeling what I thought was love, if only for a few minutes. So, he had his girlfriends, and I had my boos. But we did what we did as often as we could.

Senior year was finally here. I graduated by the skin of my teeth. But before graduation was prom. I had already decided against my better judgement to not go straight to college. I called myself wanting to take a break first. I just wanted to have fun and, more so, numb the pain. I was already drinking, and smoking weed heavily.

Me and Bestie were still together all the time and did everything together still. By second semester of our senior year, we had dropped every class we didn't need to graduate. We would leave school around 11:30 to spend the rest of the day getting high or spending some guy's money. Back then, we thought it was cute to be seen with an older guy. We would often have older guys pick us up from school or my house, not knowing at the time they were pedophiles.

I guess we didn't see anything wrong with it because they were usually about three or four years older than us. I'm sure the molestation played a part for me.

So, we were 17 and that would make them 21 or 22. The oldest guys we dealt with back then were about 27 and 28, but again, we thought it was cute. We didn't realize we were victims.

On prom night, Bestie and I left prom early, separated for a couple of hours, and met back at her room to smoke. I ended up getting so high, I fell asleep in her room.

Her prom date was pissed and so was mine as I had left him in our hotel room overnight and alone. I didn't go back to my room until about 5 am.

Graduation Day is a blur. I remember walking across the stage and feeling so thankful as I honestly didn't deserve to walk.

I had missed too many days, skipping, and had it not been for my doctor (who just so happened to be a friend of the family), I would have failed due to attendance. Sometimes you have to know somebody that knows somebody by the grace of GOD.

Bestie and I were so high on graduation day that we missed all the cookouts and off to college parties. I didn't have a concrete plan, and at the time, didn't understand or realize how much I needed one.

It was June of 1999, after graduation and a night of "entertaining" some male friends. I slept with one of my male friends. Then...

I missed my period!

Two weeks later, fresh out of high school, barely legal, with no money and no plan, I had a baby on the way.

PART TWO

AUTUMN

"Anyone who thinks fallen leaves are dead has never watched them dancing on a windy day."
— Shira Tamir

Shit was real now!

I felt lost, scared, and confused. Wishing I had listened to my mama. I had to make a decision and make it quick. It didn't take long for me to realize that I was gonna keep my baby. Even though I was broke, with only a high school diploma, I thought I would be ok.

There was just one dilemma though… I wasn't sure who was my baby's father.

I had slept with my prom date on prom night and another guy a week later. I wasn't no Jerry Springer chick though. I told them both, "Hey, I slept with you and then you and I don't know."

The most recent guy I slept with wanted to be in a relationship, knowing the possibility. I was happy during my pregnancy. I had an amazing glow.

And I had the support of my mama, Bestie, my guy, and my family and friends. I gave birth to a healthy 7-pound 10 oz baby girl in Feb of 2000. And three months later (yes, it took that long, technology was not where it is today), I found out that my guy was indeed the father.

After the birth of my first daughter, it was imperative for me to instill self-confidence within her.

My family was full of love but didn't understand the detriment of the innocent teasing. It affected me in ways they probably still wouldn't understand and may be mad that I wrote about it.

I'm not implying that they are bad people because none of them are! It was innocent but hurtful!

So, I gave her a nickname that I still call her today so that she would know how beautiful she is no matter what anyone else said or thought. When I laid eyes on her, it was the moment I knew that I had to be beautiful too.

My prom date's family was slightly disappointed as we all thought that, by the dates, he was the father. My guy and I made it official. I got my first apartment a month before my 19th birthday, and two weeks later, my baby daddy moved in.

We were young and thought we were in love, but it didn't take long for petty arguments and drama to start. We had normal boyfriend/girlfriend drama that turned into baby daddy/baby mama drama a little too often.

He decided to go in the military so we could get out of Virginia and start a new life. We talked about marriage and set a date. I got cold feet and backed out. I wasn't in love with him—I was in love with the thought of being in love.

I felt like I had to marry him as he was the first guy to love me for me. And what if he was the only guy to love me? I didn't want to be a statistic neither. So, eventually, I gave in.

He left for the army, and I stayed in Virginia with our daughter while he went to basic training and then school. When I moved into my own place, I met a new friend. She had a baby boy a couple of months before my daughter, and we became close. Our babies were friends and so were we. I went natural, did the big chop, and started wrapping my hair like Erykah Badu.

My new friend and I started our spiritual journey together. We became closer because of the kids. Bestie and I were still tight, but things were a little different because I was in a relationship and had a kid, and she wasn't and didn't.

She still came by to hang out and I was usually free on the weekends. My aunt and uncle would keep baby girl just about every weekend, and if my aunt and uncle didn't watch her, my baby cousins did.

After my baby daddy and I discussed marriage and set a date, my new friend, my fiancé's best friend and I drove to Kentucky to attend my fiancé's graduation from basic training.

We had planned to get married the next afternoon at the local park. He was leaving for AIT (military school) the following day. My new friend and hubby's bestie watched baby girl so we could have some alone time. I got up the next morning and had to say goodbye!

I was now a 20-year-old wife and mother.

While my now husband was in school, he suffered from separation anxiety and had a very hard time with being away from me and his daughter. He also had an older son from a high school relationship.

His commander pulled some strings and got us military housing early. Hubby was still in school, so this was out of the norm.

I left my apartment and hopped on a plane with just my daughter and our clothes. We planned to come back for the furniture and belongings later as the military would pay for the move. He wanted me and his daughter there as soon as possible. So, we up and left.

We arrived in El Paso, Texas in the dead middle of the summer. We had a nice two-bedroom house on base the opposite side of the school.

Texas life was different, and two months after being there, I experienced my first sandstorm. Back in Virginia, the storm was in formation but the stress and strains of that Texas wind... whoa, child!

Hubby thought he was getting back pay from the army, but it was advanced pay. The whole month of August and the first pay period of September we were flat broke.

Cell phones were cut off for non-payment so I couldn't call home. No food with a 10-month-old baby. I didn't know what to do.

They say God never puts more on us than we can handle, and he always gives us a way out.

Hubby's school was all the way on the other side of the base. I put my daughter in her stroller and walked around the neighborhood. I was confused and afraid.

As I was walking, an older woman whom I would call an Angel asked me if I was ok. I broke down.

She grabbed me, hugged me, and told me everything would be ok. Her daughter-in-law, who soon became my friend, put me and baby girl in her car and we drove to Hubby's barracks to find out what I could do.

He was upset to learn there was nothing that could be done.

His friends gave him money to give me to hold us over. I used my new friend's phone to call home for help. She took us to the commissary and invited us to eat dinner with them that night.

We became super close after that. She was the blackest white girl I know. She could cook her ass off, was married to a black guy, and would braid baby girl's hair. Loyal, real, and we had the ultimate similarity of not being afraid to smack fire out of anyone that disrespected us.

When we discovered we both smoked weed, it was over. We became newfound besties. We shopped, partied, and cooked meals together.

She had a little girl a couple of months older than my daughter and they would play together. We became so close, our husbands became friends, and we potty-trained our little girls together.

We would have good times in the front yard (on a military base, we were bold, and that was about 20+ years ago), smoking and drinking and listening to music. She showed me around El Paso as she had already been there a year. We were two wild young military wives out in Texas, living our lives!

Life in Texas was a big ass sandstorm.

Ups and downs filled with frustrations caused by insecurities. Immaturity mixed with childhood trauma. We had a lot of growing up to do.

Baby boy was born after we thought we were ready to add an addition to the family, but the wind was still blowing as the fighting didn't stop. Our honeymoon stage didn't last long as things between us began to get physical.

Sometimes I would provoke him and even hit him first. He would hit me out of anger after catching me in a lie or if I had been caught doing whorish activities. See, he wasn't always the bad guy.

I was young and didn't realize that it was not his job to make or keep me happy.

I was lost, broken, and confused, thinking that I had to have a man love me in order to be happy. And then there's that statistic thing again.

Things with us were not always bad. We did have good times but the bad outweighed the good.

I left him and came back to Virginia during my second pregnancy. At seven months, we decided to give our love another try, and I went back to Texas to work on my marriage and rekindle my family.

With me having a new baby, we were granted bigger base housing. After my son was born, the physical dysfunctions were amplified. I don't think he understood post-partem, and with it being my second baby and me being so young and uneducated, I don't think I understood it either.

One day, we got into a big argument that turned physical. I was left with black eyes, a busted blood vessel, and bruises on my body and face. The military was involved this time and he was restricted to the barracks and given extra duty assignments.

By now, my newfound bestie had moved out of state. Their time in El Paso was up. I didn't get close to anyone else after they moved away. She and I maintained contact and we communicate to this day via social media.

I didn't have to make a new friend because, not long after that, he was discharged from the military.

We were broke, unhappy, and homeless with two babies.

Well, this sandstorm was something I thought I would never get out of.

Having to move back to Virginia with nothing but our children and a car with a note we could not afford, we ended up moving in with my mother.

I got a job at a local call center and worked my ass off to provide and take care of the kiddos. He worked various low-end jobs to help make ends meet but nothing solid.

Not long after, I was offered an apartment in one of the housing authorities. Two bedrooms in a place I always told myself I would never live in, let alone raise two children in. This is where and when I had to learn to be humble!

Hubby and I were still unhappy.

We even tried to spice up our sex life to make it better, only to make it worse. The infidelity became almost the norm for me as I was still looking for love in all the wrong places and ways. Yep, even with a husband. I still felt a void.

This, I'm sure, made his heart not only cold but hard. This physical altercation was bad. I was clotheslined by the clothesline... literally!

I was knocked unconscious by the clothesline and woke up to a worried husband and an ice pack. We stopped fighting but only for a little while!

One day, I got a knock on my door from the rental office, asking if I would like to be transferred to a three-bedroom. I accepted the offer with uttermost excitement.

We had a conversation yet again about making our relationship work. We moved in, set up, and settled in… and then he lost his job.

We had already lost the car due to an accident that he was in, causing total loss. So, I was catching rides or the bus.

One day, Mama gets a phone call.

It was my Godfather with some bad news.

Mama calls me and says… "Your father has cancer."

Ok, wait… should I care? I mean, he was never there for me.

But I did care. I made the necessary call and went to see my daddy.

He seemed to be in high spirits. We would talk and laugh. I would show him pictures of the kids trying to catch him up on what he missed.

He was in and out of the hospital. Fighting.

He fought hard until the end.

As it got close, I begged him to fight. I told him I loved him and needed him to fight for me.

He cried and promised that he would. I can still hear the crying and his voice in my head.

Two days later, six months after diagnosis, my daddy passed away.

I felt a range of emotions from anger to abandonment to guilt.

I was mad at God.

"Why did you finally give him to me, just to take him right back. HOW DARE YOU!"

Hubby was supportive when my father passed but I couldn't sit in my grief too long.

He still didn't have a solid gig.

So, I got a job as a server at a restaurant where the employees felt like family. I loved working there.

While working on the marriage, we decided it was time for baby number three. I was super excited for a new bundle of joy but had a miscarriage due to complications. Now, the sand is in my damn eye. I'm in a deep depression.

Again…

I wouldn't say we tried again, but without preventing it, I was pregnant again a couple of months later. This pregnancy was complicated, but I was able to deliver my second baby girl, my third child in April of 2006. I still wasn't happy though!

After baby number three, I surrounded myself with what I thought was friends. One of them was, but the other more of an opportunist.

The two of them decided to hash out their beef in my living room. I was very fond of these two friends, so for them to disrespect my home and my children was a shocker for me.

One night after work at the restaurant, one of my cousins (who also worked there) decided to go to my house for a little after work wind down. My cousin was not too fond of Hubby because, in her opinion, he was a bum. So, her respect for him was slim to none.

They got into a heated argument.

She said something he didn't like and honestly pissed him off. All hell broke loose when he took it upon himself to put his hands on my cousin.

That incident caused a lot of unnecessary drama with my family as I had just had a baby by C-section and didn't choose a side. In other words, I just watched the scene play out in total shock and didn't do anything but stand there yelling, "STOP!"

Drama, drama, and more DRAMA!

My cousin and I's relationship became distant as she felt I should have done something... like leave his ass. But I didn't.

The fighting physically and arguing continued but I still couldn't find the strength to leave. I still didn't want to break up my family no matter how toxic it was. I was doing it for my babies... so I thought.

The unhappiness I felt was not enough to make me leave until I found someone else. I just knew the grass would be greener on the other side, but it wasn't. It was artificial as hell!

PART THREE

WINTER

"To appreciate the beauty of a snowflake, it is necessary to stand out in the cold."
— Aristotle

The biggest storm of my life!

Baby girl was four months old now. I hadn't lost all the weight from having her yet so let's say I was feeling myself.

My favorite season is spring, not only for the weather but it's the season where I'm the happiest.

On my off days from the restaurant, I would walk around the neighborhood for exercise and fresh air or walk to the store for snacks for the kids or a Pepsi for myself. I was still living in the place I thought I never would.

On a warm and bright spring day, I decided to walk to the store with baby girl in her stroller. I knew a couple of people in the area but usually stayed to myself.

I got up that morning feeling pretty good. On my way to the store, I was approached by a guy. He was the finest man I had ever been approached by… my heart began to race, and I stuttered telling him my name.

I thought to myself, "Girllllla"! This has never happened before and, hell, your ass is married, abort mission!"

So, I flirted for about 10 minutes and continued my journey to the store with baby girl. He asked for my number.

I respectfully declined.

A couple of weeks went by and I took another walk, but this time, alone. Hubby and I were not getting along as I was frustrated with his unemployment and lack of wanting to handle his responsibilities.

I saw the same guy. He approached me, but this time, against my better judgment, I gave him my number. He called the next day while I was at work.

I got those butterflies when he told me who he was. I quickly dismissed the call as I was in the middle of my serving shift at the restaurant. I promised to call him back. I felt guilty later as Hubby and I started to rebuild. So, I never called.

Things were starting to turn around for me and Hubby. He got a good job, was helping more around the house, and just overall being a better husband, yet I still felt incomplete.

I was still unhappy!

I found myself wanting to be at work more often as work became a crutch to hide my unhappiness at home. I started to party more, drink more often, and smoke more weed.

I simply didn't want to be a wife or mother anymore.

A couple of months later, on my way to the hair store, I saw old boy. I approached him this time.

I said, "Hey, what's up, you don't call me no more."

He said, "For what? You just gonna keep brushing me off."

I replied, "No, I'm not. Call me this weekend so we can link."

He said, "Yeah, alright."

I worked a double that weekend with my cousin. He called my phone about 10 pm.

"Yo, what's up, shorty, I'm trying to see you."

I replied, "Dats what's up, when and where?"

He said, "I'm round the way. Imma text u my address."

I said, "Well, Imma have to come when I get off."

He said, "Oh, that's cool."

I rushed to wrap up my night to get to the man of my dreams... so I thought!

Cuzzo dropped me off and told me to have a good night, be careful, and not get caught. She laughed and then left. Mr. Wrong decided to roll a blunt and offered me a drink.

I drank up and smoke about two blunts with him.

He suggested that I take off my shoes and relax. I was fresh off work and sneaking so I didn't go home and shower first.

That made me a little insecure.

He said, "No, you're good, get comfortable."

So, I did.

He offered to give me a foot and back massage.

I didn't decline.

He then suggested I take another shot and a quick shower. So, I did. After the shower, he gave me a massage.

Without hesitation, and against my vows and morals, I slept with Mr. Wrong.

As expected, I didn't hear from him for about two weeks. I wasn't surprised or disappointed as, again, it was expected.

I knew what I was doing.

I hadn't seen him for about two months.

I approached him like he owed me something.

He laughed and said, "Chill. I didn't want to disrespect your marriage."

I replied, "That's for me to worry about, and if I ain't worried, you shouldn't be either."

He said, "Oh, word then."

He called that weekend. This time, I stayed the night.

After about six months, I decided the grass was perfectly green and I no longer wanted my husband.

Mr. Wrong got put out of his people's place. I decided to put Hubby out and, two weeks later, allowed Mr. Wrong to move in.

Hubby didn't like it and was extremely hurt. I didn't care. Selfish of me. I wanted what I wanted.

Things were ok in the beginning.

Although Mr. Wrong didn't claim me, he was telling people in the neighborhood that we were just friends and that I was just helping him out. I still wanted to be with him.

That was definitely a red flag, but I let it slip by.

He was different, and even though he was not claiming me, I didn't want for anything financially. Me or the kids, and at the time, I was ok with that.

About two or three months into our situationship, Mr. Wrong started claiming me out of the blue.

Looking back, I think it was more so because people in the neighborhood started putting two and two together. Nonetheless, he was calling me his lady and spoiling me and my kids. When the song, "Throw it in the Bag" came out, you would have thought it was my theme song.

If I didn't want to cook, I didn't have to.

If we went to the mall and I wanted something, it was… "Boo, throw it in the bag!"

It wasn't long before I started hearing rumors and then I started to find numbers in his jeans when I washed his clothes, late-night text messages and calls.

Then I started finding condoms in his pocket and wallet when ours were in the bedside nightstand. He would give me little boy excuses and dumb-ass reasons as to why he had numbers and condoms. I didn't believe him, and with all these red flags, I didn't end it.

I was more concerned about the *I told you so's* I would hear from my baby daddy, friends and family. So, I lied to myself and told myself that if I wanted to be with an attractive, get money nigga, this was what I would have to deal with.

I would half-ass break up with him out of anger but never stuck to my word. He had a way with his words, money, and sex that made me overlook the storm I was getting ready to put myself in.

Month after month, I would find out about another chick. Some nights, he wouldn't come home at all. That still didn't make me leave. I started to regret breaking up my family just to still be unhappy, but then Mr. Wrong would give another nice gesture and all was forgiven.

Cheating, cheating, and more cheating. He even cheated with a man and that still didn't make me leave.

I was so weak. And pathetically weak for him. It's what happens when you lose yourself in a person and you love them more than yourself.

All wasn't bad with Mr. Wrong either.

I met a lot of cool-ass down-to-earth people as him and his family was very popular. People I didn't even know would walk up to me and say, "Hey, ain't you Mr. Wrong's girl..."

I would say, "Yeah," and get freeways in the club, free weed... all kinda lookouts. People knew not to fuck with me off the name of who my boyfriend was.

He and my baby daddy even got into a couple of fights behind my ex still claiming me as his wife... I was, but Mr. Wrong made it very clear that I was his girl, and this was his family now.

I lost some friends behind my decision, and my part in breaking up what the world thought was my happy home. And when I tried to explain my reasons as to why, that wasn't good enough for them.

They would say, "Girl, that shit doesn't matter, he is still your husband and you're still wrong." I wasn't trying to hear that. After all, I was happy, and they needed to mind their business, even if I was dead wrong. I later wished I had taken their advice.

Being with Mr. Wrong made me sick.

Literally.

I have always been thin, but I was down to a 0 in clothes. I had lost my little shape and confidence too. I cried all the time and was still very depressed.

He was outwardly cheating at this point and the stability he provided in the beginning was no longer there. We had moved out of public housing as my apartment had become hot. He was the weed man in the hood and surrounding neighborhood.

He moved the kids and I into a house. That didn't last long either. We bounced around a lot. I would cry to his family often and they would question me as to why I would stay. I still don't know the answer. I guess I thought I loved him that much. And maybe I did. Or I didn't. I didn't love myself. He would even mess with girls in the hood—chicks I saw every day.

Because weed was something I didn't have to spend money on... I smoked a lot.

It got to a point where I was so numb that the things he did didn't bother me anymore. I caught a weed charge and was put on first-offender status. I was to report to CCD once a month for three months to make sure the charge didn't end up on my record. I tried everything one could think of to pass the piss test except STOP smoking... epic fail!

I pissed dirty every time. I got pulled over. My lawyer talked the judge into adding the driving charge to my CCD.

A year passed and nothing changed with Mr. Wrong. I still wanted and needed to smoke to numb the pain. I eventually told CCD I was done with the program and to just give me the damn charge.

Forgetting about the driving charge, the judge ordered me to a 90-day drug program in Newport News City Jail.

During that 90-day period, Mr. Wrong met a chick and got her pregnant.

I came home to him introducing me to K2—a drug he described as fake weed. It was a very addictive and dangerous drug that gave the effect of marijuana. The storm was brewing. After the first hit. I was hooked.

All was forgiven with the girl who was pregnant, the dick pics, the chat lines, and all the other chicks… as long as I had the K2.

He was very conniving and absolutely condescending. He told her he was a basketball player at HU and the baby would mess up his career. He convinced her to have an abortion.

Then we got evicted again. This time, because I was in jail for three months, I couldn't save us. I was working but didn't have anything saved. I sent the kids with my mom and Mr. Wrong and I slept where we could or with whoever would let us get their floor for the night. Nothing and no one mattered but K2 and Mr. Wrong.

Most of the time, we would usually get upset with our parents for discussing our business with other people, but in this instance, I wasn't upset at all.

When I met my new friend, whom we will call Doll Face, I wasn't upset at all. It was as if we already knew each other, mostly because we knew each other's business.

Our mothers are best friends and would vent to each other about their daughters and what they were experiencing at the moment.

So, when I met Doll Face in person, I already knew what she was going through, and she knew my story too. It was as if we automatically clicked. Our significant others at the time (Mr. Wrong and Hell Raiser) were narcissistic deadbeats, so we could automatically relate.

We would work out the toxic relationships we were in and later introduce Mr. Wrong and Hell Raiser to each other. They became friends and put us through all the shenanigans and buffoonery that you could possibly think of.

This, however, made our bond even stronger. I consider her a best friend today as she is one of the people I can go to about anything with no judgement and no negativity.

Plus, she's funny and talented too.

She eventually left Hell Raiser. Mr. Wrong and Hell Raiser are still stuck in the same spots we left them. Mama always said a leopard can't change its spots.

Doll Face and I have grown in more ways than we can be thankful for. I appreciate her being a part of my story. The good and the bad.

Now, back to Mr. Wrong…

At one point, I'd had enough. I prayed and begged God to remove Mr. Wrong from my life. I got an apartment for the kids and myself.

It was a new beginning, so to speak. I stayed strong for about three months until he started calling and I gave in. Doll Face and Hell Raiser moved in with us for a while and those two put us through more than you can imagine. And we were too weak to leave.

Bestie lived behind us. I'm sure she got sick of me beating down her door and crying behind the things he would do. The cheating, the lies, the stealing, the down-low behavior… all of it

Things were going great as he was spoiling me and the kids again. We were both working, and he was hustling. The work for him didn't last long. He was more concerned with hustling than going to work, and entertaining females with his lies and hunts of opportunity, so he lost his job.

I picked up a gig as a dancer to hold down his portion.

Fourth of July weekend, there was a shooting.

A guy was shot in our parking lot, ran around the corner, and collapsed right off my back patio.

We went into panic mood as he was still hustling, so we turned off all the lights and pretended to not be home. We knew the police were definitely on their way.

I was uncomfortable with being in the area with my children and started to plan to move. I found a house, owned by a nice Christian couple who were willing to give us a chance. Besides, Mr. Wrong was a master manipulator who could talk a great game.

We paid the deposit and moved in a month later. We both got jobs at the same location with no definite way to get there. My grandmother was no longer driving and sold her car to my older cousin, and we purchased the car from him to get to work.

One day, Mr. Wrong was about to get stopped by the police… let's keep in mind this douchebag was still hustling. He decided to run from the police who were trying to pull him over for speeding. He wrecked the car and ran. I guess God was on his side because, somehow, his ass got away. He then began paying his homeboy to drive him around. That's when he met her!

Months went by and nothing got better—only worse. The cheating continued, but this time, I knew the chick… a snowstorm is brewing!

Before I allowed life circumstances and no-good-men to drain me of my confidence and esteem, I always felt I was thin enough to model. When I was approached by a guy that had started his own modeling agency, I then felt confident.

I started to model with this group of women. We would go to a studio to practice. The group was clicked up and, as usual, I wasn't a part of the click.

Homewrecker and I were cool but not friends. We knew of each other through group members but didn't hang out unless it was modeling related.

I was nice to everyone though. Some didn't have cars, so me and a friend of mine that was also modeling would give the members rides to and from practice and/or events. Homewrecker and I would talk, but as I previously stated, we were not friends.

While I was trying to find my lane with modeling, Mr. Wrong was out fucking up money he claimed to be hustling.

I started dancing at another exotic club to make ends meet, which meant I wasn't getting home until about 3 am. That, of course, gave Mr. Wrong the chance to keep doing what he was doing and more often.

I had not caught him in a while, so at the time, I felt we were good. Out of the blue, his behavior started to display signs from before. But this time, he was bold. I would always go through his phone, and I really found what I was looking for. I read the messages and listened to the voicemails, and it all started to make sense.

I, of course, went off to be punched in the face for invading privacy. But what I read and heard crushed me more. It was some chick I will call "Q", the Homewrecker, telling him how much she enjoyed the time and the sex they had...

Huh... SEX?

So, I called myself being a woman and calling to have a conversation with this broad but was immediately made to feel stupid.

Me: "Hi, this is Dee… I'm calling you because I read some messages in my man's phone and listened to his voicemail. I'm just calling you like a woman to let you know we're in a committed relationship. And so, I'm trying to figure out what's going on with y'all?"

The Homewrecker: "Girl… (starts laughing). You need to question him if that's your man."

Me: "No, I'm coming to you like a woman because niggas lie. I'm just trying to protect my heart. I have kids, he's been in my youngest kid's life since she was 10 months old, so I'm asking you."

The Homewrecker: "Well, you need to ask him."

Then I heard the dial tone.

I went after him first. Question after question was answered with lie after lie.

First, he didn't even know a "Q", then she was a customer, then it's his homeboys' people, then… "Oh I do know her, she been on my dick for a while."

I was used to the lies, abuse, and cheating I thought, but this one hit different once I kept digging.

He just didn't seem to care and, eventually, didn't even hide it. I still didn't leave as, at the time, I felt like she would win. The back and forth between the two of us continued for about two or three weeks and I discovered that the homewrecker, Ms. Q, was, in fact, a girl I was modeling with.

The same one I had given plenty of rides to, laughed with, and never thought for a minute would go behind my back. This chick knew exactly who I was and who Mr. Wrong was to me. She ain't give a damn either.

The back-and-forth text messages and calls lasted for about a week. I was crushed and angry.

Livid to be exact.

I started back on the spice heavy. But was still trying to fight the demon to be a better person.

On a sunny fall morning, I decided to stop feeling sorry for myself and get him off my mind by going to a job fair. I got up, got dressed, and called my cousin. I made sure to calm my nerves by smoking just a little of the same spice Mr. Wrong had introduced me to. I went to pick her up. We were in mid-convo when I got a blocked call. I didn't answer at first, but the second blocked call made me pick up.

When I answered the phone, at first, I didn't hear anything. I kept saying, "Hello?" Then I heard the moans. This crazy-ass chick had called me while they were having sex. I hung up, pulled over, and screamed. I felt taunted, hopeless, as she had taken MY man.

Then I got a text: "I got your man, and we got plans."

I called Mr. Wrong's phone, and she answered, laughing, and then told me, "Bitch pull up." She sent the address and I fell right into the trap.

THE STORM

I got to her apartment, livid.

I got out of the SUV and went to knock on her door. A friend of hers opened the door, immediately talking shit. I went down the stairs and invited Q to fight.

She started throwing things at me. A pot of grease off the stove, a Mountain Dew bottle, and some more. I started to throw things back at her.

I got so angry, I started to not feel like myself anymore. The last thing I remember is getting back into the truck. I had never had an out-of-body experience before, so I didn't know what I was doing. I was later told this was the chain of events:

My cousin and I got back into the truck to get ready to leave. I put the truck in reverse and said:

ME: "I'm about to run this bitch over."

My cousin: "Na, cuz, you can't do that, you might hurt her and it's broad daylight."

ME: "I don't give a fuck."

Oh, how I wish I did give a fuck. I did just what I said I was going to do. I put the truck in reverse and hit the gas. I drove over the curb and, boom, I hit someone or something.

I heard screams.

I snapped back into reality, and when I looked around, I was in disbelief.

I had hit an innocent bystander trying to break up the fight. He had stepped in the truck's path as I was attempting to hit Q.

I put the truck in reverse and hauled ass out of the complex with my heart beating a million miles a minute, all while my cousin was frantically screaming, "What did you do, why did you do that?" I didn't answer, I just drove.

We got back to her house, and I washed the truck. I went home and changed clothes. Rolled me a blunt of spice and sat on the porch. My phone started to ring off the hook. I finally answered and it was Mr. Wrong.

Mr. Wrong: "OMG, YO, you killed that man, you're going to jail."

Me: "I should have killed your ass, fuck you!"

I turned my phone off. Mama came home from work (I was living with her at the time) and asked me if what she heard was true. I lied and said no, and she said, "I figured his ass was lying."

The next morning, I called off work. My oldest child was sick, so I stayed home with her. We were in the den playing Monopoly when there was a knock on the door.

"HAMPTON POLICE, OPEN UP!"

I had already told my aunt (Doll Face's mom—my mom's best friend) what happened, and she immediately became Erica Cane… "No, Ms. Adkinson is not home."

I went to hide in the closet.

The officer asked if he could search the home.

I don't know if it was the grace of God or if the officer didn't want to take me in front of my oldest, but I did not get apprehended that day. I put my head in the back of the closet and my shoulders up against the bars like I was hanging clothes.

Either way, I was safe… for now.

Ok, so I realized I was in deep shit. I mean, I knew it happened, but I guess I thought if I didn't think about it, it would go away.

I got out of the closet and packed as much as I could in a small book bag and a small duffle bag. Before I could get out of the door, Mama came home. I had to tell the truth this time as I had a warrant for my arrest.

I have never seen my mama cry in my 31 years of life. I kissed her and walked out of her room. I gave my aunt instructions on what to do with my children.

I called a friend that lived outside the area and told her I was in trouble. She asked if I could get somewhere safe until she got off work. I told her yes, so I went to a homeboy's house until she could come and get me.

About 10:30 pm, she got to me. I thanked and hugged my friend and we drove off. I sat in the back of her car and cried the whole one-and-a-half-hour drive to her house.

I was distraught, angry, and disappointed with myself. I realized that my life would be different from that point on. I had thrown my life away for a man.

I couldn't sleep. I called everyone out outside of Virginia, I was scared and decided I was going on the run. After explaining what happened, no one outside of Virginia was willing to get involved. So, I stayed with my friend for about a week.

One day, I got a phone call from a 757 number, being that I had called Mr. Wrong a couple of times crying and asking why, to only hear laughs and jokes about how I was going to jail, and they would live their best lives while I was away, I assumed it was him. But it was Big Bro.

He told me to go and turn myself in. He promised to have my back and help me get a lawyer, but I had to make the first step. I was so scared of what would happen to me that I didn't go right away. I did come back to the Hampton Roads area and stayed with Bro for a week.

I finally mustered up enough courage to go and turn myself in. I smoked an entire pack of cigarettes to calm my nerves as I didn't know what to expect. It was a cold, gloomy night. I turned to kiss my friend on the cheek and said my goodbyes.

That moment was the beginning of my new life—behind bars.

I walked into the jail, told them my name, signed the necessary paperwork, and was politely walked to the holding area. I was feeling pretty positive as my family hired a reputable lawyer. I intended to ride it out. I sent a request to the overseer of a drug program called inner reflections—the same program I had previously completed while in jail before. I would be moved to the drug block about two months after I turned myself in.

The drug program was on the cleaner side of the jail. Because this was the second time in the program, I knew what to expect. I also knew the privileges of the program would make my stay a little more comfortable.

I had the chance to begin to get my power back, but this time, I didn't take the program seriously. I was still worried and concerned about what Mr. Wrong was doing in the streets, listening and still believing the lies he would tell me.

I looked forward to Friday nights, which were visitation. Mr. Wrong would visit with more promises and more lies. He did manage to keep a little money on my books. My mom and Bestie would visit too.

The inner reflections program was only 90 days. 11 pm was lights out. Two days after I finished the program, at about one in the morning, a guard yelled, "Adkinson, pack up."

I got off my rack and began to pack my things. I passed out some commissary to a couple of people I knew didn't have anyone on the outside looking out, then pressed the call button and was escorted back to the main prison holding cell. I was confused. I asked a deputy why I was in the bullpen (that's what they call the holding cell in this particular jail… if you know, you know) and was told I was being transferred out. I wasn't expecting that. The next morning, I was moved to the Peninsula Regional Jail.

Now this was different.

I had never stepped foot in this place before. It was bigger, with more people, guards, and inmates. The food was better though, and the commissary, but this place was like a baby prison. Extremely strict rules.

The day I was processed, the jail just so happened to be on "lock down". I learned that lock down consisted of being in your cell 24 hours a day for three days to a week. However long it took them to shake the whole jail down for contraband. Contraband, for those that don't know, is all items restricted in jail. Even items that incarcerated individuals would make out of their own creativity. All three meals were given through a slit in the door. Showers were given at random and at the deputy's discretion.

This shit was too much.

Recreation was still inside of the building in another section of the jail. I was not used to this as Newport News City Jail's inner reflections program, we were allowed to go outside and get some fresh air at least three to four times a week. Depending on which deputies were on shift, we would go out twice in one day.

Outside air gave me much-needed rejuvenation, even under the circumstances. At the Regional, recreation consisted of a rubber gym floor and a basketball goal. The men usually had the option of the weight room.

I ran into some familiar faces when I didn't expect to know anyone. I met some cool people there too—believe it or not. I knew the routine of NNCJ but not this place. I was lucky enough to connect with some older ladies who schooled me on how to get by.

My bunkmate was a girl from Norfolk who was also on her way to prison. I hadn't been sentenced yet or even went to trial, but I knew my fate. My bunky, however, was just waiting for the DOC bus to pull up and her number to be called.

She was serving a seven-year sentence for arson. This was her second time setting some shit on fire. She was nice though. Always tried to share where I would respectfully decline as she loved to dig in her nose. She was a little special, but again, super nice. She also helped me learn a little more about that place.

One day, we were in the recreation area. If you have ever seen Paid in Full, remember the scene where Mitch was in the jail... that's exactly how the Regional is designed to give you a sort of visual.

I was on the phone with my back to everyone. I didn't hear the bell or the deputies yelling for everyone to go to their assigned cells. I was deep in my phone call, telling my mom I was ready for a bond hearing. I was having a hard time in this place.

The next thing I know, I was being yanked from the phone and thrown to the ground. I dropped the phone, of course. Deputy hung it up and was yelling at me at the top of his lungs. I was pinned to the ground at this point. I lifted my head to see my bunky on the ground too. Now I was thinking, what the hell? Deputy yanked me off the ground and damn near carried me to the sergeant's office.

They immediately started yelling at me, asking what the hell was my problem. I was stupid confused and scared shitless. They threatened me with the red suit (red suits were given to inmates that bucked. Whether it be fighting, disrespecting a guard, being in an unauthorized area (like someone else's cell), or contraband, etc. I was so upset because I could not figure out what I had done wrong.

The sergeant started to explain that I should have been in my cell when the bell went off and deputies were yelling at everyone. Through tears, I explained I had never been there before and the jail I came from was nothing like this.

Because of my charges, I assume, he wasn't buying it. I was restricted to my cell for three days. No phone calls, no commissary, no rec room.

Come to find out my crazy ass bunky was known for bucking. She thought I was bucking by not getting off the phone. She was behind me going crazy thinking she was following me. She got three days restriction too. The whole time, my ass was just on the phone.

I intended to ride this thing out, but after this and being fed up with boogers all over the walls and door in my cell, I'd had enough, so after my three days of restriction, I called my mom and told her to call my lawyer and set the bond hearing. I was ready to go.

I got a bond hearing about two weeks later. I had to travel back to NN to go to court. Being handcuffed and shackled to be put on a bus was all the punishment I needed to feel like I had learned my lesson. But this was just the beginning.

My prayers were answered, and I was awarded a $30,000 bond. I had to pay $3000 to get out. My backbone (my mama) made that happen. And in two days, I was walking out of jail. Free for the moment.

I couldn't shake Mr. Wrong's ass though. He was my drug and I had to have him. I know, I know, you're probably like how the hell could you possibly even think about dealing with him after all he did? Well, love is love… or so I thought.

He was putting money on my books (well, her money) and coming to see me every Friday, so I fell back into the trap. Against Mama's wishes, I continued to be with him, sleep with him, and sneak him into her house to do it. I was the only one convinced that he had "changed", and rightfully so.

Out on bond, we picked up where we left off. If I couldn't sneak him into Mama's house, I would meet him other places or get a room for the night.

He had this hold on me that I just couldn't shake. Months went by without me being focused. All I could think about was him. I neglected my children, family, and friends just to be with him.

Months went by and I went out on bond in May. I had my lawyer push my case back for as long and as far as possible. Looking back, I guess I just didn't want to face it. I was scheduled back to court in Jan of 2012. A year had gone by just that quickly.

January 04, 2012, I decided to marry Mr. Wrong, four days before my scheduled sentencing hearing.

Homie #1's cousin took us to the justice of the peace to help us make this happen. And on Jan 08, 2012, Mama dropped us off at court. She was not feeling well. My lawyer had a plan for a motion to dismiss as the prosecutor's key witness had changed her story, so I kissed Mama's cheek and sent her home. I told her I would see her later. In normal circumstances, Mama would have showed face anyway, but honestly, I think she was overwhelmed, scared, and tired.

I stood before a judge, nervous as a hooker in church.

He was a substitute judge, so I was already thinking negatively.

My lawyer gave his argument and called my witnesses to the stand. Total disaster as one was Mr. Wrong's lying ass. The judge cut all the shenanigans short. He told my lawyer, "Nice try, wise guy, but I feel like you're just trying to get a second bite of the apple, you should have done this at the trial. Ms. Adkinson will be sentenced today!"

My heart dropped!

It was sort of like I was a character on Charlie Brown when his parents were on the phone.

I was sentenced to 11 years in prison on the malicious wounding charge, all suspended, but one year and nine months on the hit and run, all suspended, but nine months to be served concurrently. Five years supervised probation with 10 years good behavior.

To be taken into custody immediately!

I wasn't prepared for this. I didn't get to say goodbye to my babies.

The judge didn't care.

I cried, I screamed, I yelled at the top of my lungs in the holding cell. It didn't help or change a thing. I had a nice deputy come and tell me to quiet down before the judge gave me more time. I shut up real quick.

I just laid there in that cold cell, lying on the bench crying as the reality of how I had just thrown my life away began to sink in.

How could I be so dumb?

All I could do was cry.

Hours passed and then I was taken to the hold for processing. I was given my phone calls... and you know who I called first?

Yep, Mr. Wrong.

I cried as if he could save me or fix the situation. And like he didn't play a part. I listened to the promises of holding me down and never leaving me. While I wanted to believe it, I knew he was already on his way to do him. I had lost him and was more concerned about that than anyone and anything else.

I talked to Mama, who assured me the kids would be fine. I was taken up to the women's floor and told to grab a mattress and find a bed. I cried all night. It was impossible to sleep... so I just lay there and cried some more.

As soon as I fell asleep, I heard a deputy yell, "Trays, ladies." I was starving, so I got up.

For no damn reason though, food looked like throw-up, so I damn sure wasn't gonna see what it tasted like. Besides, I was exhausted, so I tried to lay back down.

What felt like five minutes later, I was startled out of my sleep by a deputy yelling and banging on the bars about count time. She even said, "On your feet." I was so irritated.

Why the hell we gotta stand up when we can't go nowhere? I thought it was just because they could until someone told me it was for safety.

I was still irritated.

Jail is not a happy place. No personal space, no boundaries, no privacy. And although I had been in that place before, there was no getting comfortable… you just have to adapt.

I managed to be moved to a calmer block for women and was able to send another request for the drug block. I had to get out of the main jail.

The drug counselor would come to the main jail at least twice a month, and when she did, I made sure I spoke with her. About a month or so later, she pulled me back to the program, but this time, with higher expectations as this would be the third time I would be in it. I promised not to let her down.

I couldn't focus on the program though. I was still too concerned with what Mr. Wrong was out there doing and counting down to Friday's visitation to see him.

I met some dope women in that program that I still associate with today. Some of them helped me in ways they have no idea. I did get some good out of the program, it wasn't only drama.

I was able to get sober and look at myself for real and seriously for the first time. I wanted to move forward and get my time over with. Between myself, my mama, and Mr. Wrong repeatedly contacting DOC, I was relocated to DOC processing two days after completing the program. I was super nervous as I was on my way to prison.

I didn't know what to think or to expect on the two-hour drive to Brunswick. That's where I did my intake. My body was tight and sore as I got out of the police car. My wrists and ankles were a little swollen from being shackled for two hours. My back and side hurt as I sat in an uncomfortable position for that long. The intake process was lengthy. They gave us bag lunches (from the jail at that) to eat while we waited.

I took my mugshot in DOC attire for my ID, got my state-issued necessities, and escorted to my assigned bunk. An open pod with like 200 beds… way less privacy than I expected. Like, where are the cells?

There were two sides to Brunswick as part of it was a work camp. Intake side, of course, had stricter rules and less commissary. The workforce side was allowed visitors and TVs, nail polish, and some other things to give them some sense of freedom.

By day three, I was completely over it. I had no commissary, and I wasn't in the system to make calls yet. Besides, there were only four phones with 200 women. Some were mothers like me and wanted to know what was going on at home more than focusing on how to better their current situation.

One day, as I was cleaning in the kitchen (a deputy noticed how clean I kept my space and asked me to help her out. That one time turned quickly into too often as I didn't mind. It helped the time go by), I saw a familiar face. I was happy to see someone I knew.

We became family there (we were already like family as we grew up in the same neighborhoods and she had a baby with one of my cousins). I cleaned the kitchen after every chow just to be able to have some conversation with someone I knew.

We talked about how much we both hated this place, how we missed our babies and family, and how we would do and be better when we left. I did meet some dope-ass women in that place and created some forever bonds too.

I did a lot of reading and writing to pass the time. When I did get phone privileges, I would burn the lines up.

We played games in the day room and listened to the pod drama. We watched the fights and ate. Commissary and eating were the best parts of intake. With being locked up for about four months now, my singing voice was strong from not smoking. I would sing and, eventually, it became a highlight for some of the women.

I was still ready to go home though.

In the wee hours of the morning, 30 days later, a group of 15-20 women were told to pack up. I jumped up at the opportunity to leave that place. I would miss my cousin but looked forward to seeing her on the other side rather than this place.

We were handcuffed and shackled and loaded onto a white bus for our next chapter. On the bus, we joked, laughed, and took turns singing old RNB songs. I had Mary J. Blige on lock and sung My Life like three times on the way.

The driver, I assume, enjoyed the concert as he and the guards didn't ask us to quiet down. So, for two and a half hours, we entertained ourselves and tried to make the best of not knowing what we would soon face. When I arrived at Fluvanna Correctional Center for Women, I didn't know it would be the beginning of my breakthrough.

Now, this place was huge. Like nothing I had ever seen. I was taken through intake, given the rules, my state-issued clothes and necessities, and walked to my pod. Building 5.

I walked in, all eyes on me. I had some women walk up to me to introduce themselves, but I was nervous as I didn't know any of them or anything about their characters.

My first roommate was cool. She was an older woman who had been there for a little over a year. She asked me what I was in for and how much time I had (I had yet to find out… you never really give anyone the real date, you just say, "I ain't got long" if it's short time, or "I'm gonna be a min" if it's really going be a min), so I told her.

She started giving me her story of how she was innocent. She gave me the details and asked me if I thought she was. I didn't care either way, so I told her, "Yeah, and you should fight." I should have just said, "Yeah," because then I had to listen to the plan of appeal for the next two hours.

She showed me the ropes. Told me which deputies were cool and which ones were assholes. The best time for phone calls and showers and how to pass the time. She asked me if I played cards. I told her yes.

"After the count clears, I will introduce you to some of the girls and we will play."

After count, it seemed like the pod went mad. I mean, we're talking about like 40 women in one room. The showers would start, and every phone would be in use.

My roommate introduced me to the girls, and we played Spades. I was just playing to play and pass some time but was dealt a good-ass hand. After the first hand bid itself, we kicked their asses with a Boston.

That was game, and from then on, everyone wanted me to be their partner… that is until my roommate told them I was "short time". I had the smallest amount of time in my pod compared to the other women, so some of them thought I thought I was better than them.

This one girl, who I thought I knew, sparked conversation with me. After talking to her, I realized I recognized her from childhood. We went to the same community center a couple of times. She was a bully back then, so I was skeptical of getting close to her. I did talk to her though.

She would show me her photo albums with familiar faces and talk about the good old days. She would cook and invite me to eat with her. The friendly conversation and free meals were all given with a motive.

If you've ever been to prison and some jails, you may have watched this video about don't eat the chips… well, I shouldn't have eaten the tuna flip.

When I would socialize, I would talk to the older women. I always felt the need to hear their wisdom, and even though I was in prison, I was interested in their stories because they had a life before prison with experiences that I could learn from and wanted to.

I tried to be cordial with all the ladies, but one girl just seemed to hate my existence. She was in the cell next to mine. She was young, beautiful, and very angry.

She was a mother also. She was a long timer with over 30 years to serve and had been incarcerated since she was a teen. She wasn't given a second chance or slapped on the wrist with short time for her mistake.

A man's life was taken, and she played a part, but to say the time given was overkill for a child is an understatement. Once I learned her story, I was able to understand her pain. I too was pissed at myself for the mistakes I made. I wanted to give her a hug and tell her things would be ok, but I made it my business to steer clear of her for the moment. I didn't know how to even approach her for conversation.

I cried myself to sleep that night, not only for my pain but hers too.

After about two months, I had put myself in a routine. I worked in the kitchen, went to church, the library, and rec whenever available. I had to stop talking to old girl as she was trying to make me her girlfriend.

I had no interest in a jailhouse relationship with her. For one, I was married and was counting down the days to be back with my family, and two, I just wasn't attracted to her. I did find a couple of studs attractive if I'm being honest and had a little crush on a couple. I just never acted on my feelings.

I played cards on occasion but usually stayed to myself. I developed a friendship with two girls. We would sit in the day room and play Three-Hand Spades or sit together as we wrote letters or just talked. Mail call was a hot commodity too.

A black cloud must have hit the pod one day because there was nothing but drama. My roommate was on one. She tried to physically fight me. I requested to be moved. I was still working in the kitchen, so I was granted a move to building 6, which was the worker's pod. I moved into a room with an old lady. She was a lifer. She was nice though. Always kind, almost like a mama.

She would share stories about her family and growing up. She talked about her son often, whom she had killed. She intentionally left him in a locked house and set the house on fire.

She said God told her to do it, and said God told her he was the antichrist. As she was telling me this story, I was scared shitless. Hell, I gotta sleep in here with her, so with fast thinking, I told her, "Thank you for killing him."

She was surprised by my response, and she said, "Wow, no one has ever said that." I was on my bunk (up top) and she was on hers... I knew my eyes were about to pop out of my head as I whispered, "You're welcome," while silently praying I was on her good side.

It was a regular day at work in the kitchen when an old pod mate (girl that was in building 5 with me and the same pod) passed me a kite (a letter, which is classified as contraband) from one of my friends from my old pod. She was apparently upset about something someone told her I said. All lies too.

The next time I saw her, we could discuss this. She worked in the kitchen too, just different hours than me. I went to lunch chow that day to specifically have this much-needed conversation with my friend.

I got through the chow line. I knew she was working the line. I bent down and asked the person in the window to tell her to come to the window. She did and I started going in, she then took the tray and mashed it into my face. I pushed back, and the next thing I know, she was coming through the side door, and we started fighting.

I'm not sure how she got through the door as it was usually locked and a guard was usually there too, but they weren't, and she did. The fight lasted about three minutes. I made sure to smack the taste out of her mouth with a tray before we were split up and hauled off to seg (segregation, the hold). Thankfully, they didn't give us any street charges or additional charges. I was sentenced to 16 days in seg. Not sure how many days she got, but I would assume about the same.

Seg was a different kind of locked up. No visitation, no commissary, no phone calls, no privileges whatsoever to make the time a little easier. One hour of rec time when the guards felt like taking us.

I used the time in seg to do some healing and getting to further know myself. I did a lot of crying, praying, reading, and writing. I wondered why I put myself in that position and what I needed to do to make sure I was never in that situation again. I began a mental plan on how to think and be different.

After my 16 days were served, I wasn't immediately released back into general population. There were no beds available, so I had to wait an additional 15 days to be put back into general population. I moved to building 1.

My new roommate seemed cool at first. The pod I was in had a lot of long-timers as well. This building also had a program where long timers were given dogs. I'm not sure what kind of program or what was the purpose of it, but I was starting to regret asking to be moved from building 5. At least I knew what to expect from the women there.

One day, my roommate and I got into it. She had a smart mouth and so did I, so it was just a matter of time before shit would hit the fan. We were close to fighting and pulled to the guard's office to discuss a solution. She was a pod worker and had been locked up for about 10 years, so she had a little bond with the deputies assigned to the pod. She suggested that I be moved to the reentry building. Neither the sergeant nor I objected. I went back to my cell to pack my things to move again.

Building 3 meant one step closer to home. I was not immediately put into the reentry program. Honestly, I didn't understand the purpose at the time and wanted the freedom of sleeping and chilling when I wanted.

I did feel a little more comfortable being around other people who were counting down their days as well. I still had a little time left and wanted to have something to show for being in prison.

I made a request for the building maintenance and repair program. I was accepted but didn't get to start the class due to the instructor getting sick. So, I sent another request for HVAC instead. I was accepted to the program. The instructor (who was a long timer who knew her stuff—I couldn't stand her either) told me on day one of my class that it would be extremely hard to complete the program and gain my certificate in the short time I had left. I was determined to prove her wrong.

A short while later, I was moved to the reentry program wing.

I was busy. And intentionally so.

The program is set up to help individuals reenter society and not return. There were a lot of mandatory classes but a lot that were not. I took every class I could too, from thinking for a change to a 12-step program to parenting. I also joined the choir and attended church.

I made up my mind early that I had a choice. I could sit around and play cards my whole bid, or TRY to better myself in the situation I was in. I began to choose to think differently.

A person was scheduled to leave the prison from that building almost every day. When the laundry tech left, I asked the lieutenant for the position. He gave it to me. So, I was focused on completing my trade and working.

Working the program—physically working—going to school for a trade, and I ran a safe space self-empowerment group that I created and ran too! The girl was busy. But it was worth it.

FINALLY!

THE SUN IS STARTING TO SHINE.

I did the laundry for my entire wing, and we were also assigned cleaning duties. Even though everyone was excited about going home soon, there was still some kind of drama in the unit. Hell, it's a pod full of women, anxious, excited, and on edge about going home soon.

I had arguments with folks, but for the most part, it was squashed before anything happened or got physical. The nonprogram wings were where most of the drama went down.

My singing voice was extremely clean, crisp, and clear. We were preparing for graduation from the program, which was a big deal. Family members and friends were allowed to come to the big day. My mom would bring hubby and the kids to come and see me every other month but could not make the graduation. I was disappointed but anxious to get out of that place.

I was asked to sing—myself and another female. We sung Hero by Mariah Carey. My voice was so loud and strong, I drowned her out unintentionally.

I met some females who would become forever friends. One I still talk to daily and the other on occasion. I will always love them and cherish the bond we had then and now.

It was time for me to go home. I was nervous, scared, and concerned about falling back into old habits, but I was determined to be a different person.

And on March 26, 2014, I was told to pack up. Oh, and I proved that instructor wrong too—I got my HVAC certification days before I was released.

In the program when it's time for you to leave, your name is on a board with your release date. And you have the option to give a little speech. I remember having to have one of my friends read my goodbye letter to the pod at that morning's meeting. I was in the bullpen watching as I received a standing ovation. I blew them all kisses, walked out of the building, and was on my way home, to a new beginning!

PART FOUR

SPRING

"Spring is God's way of saying, 'One more time!'"
— *Robert Orben*

I was released from prison on March 26, 2014, one week before my 33rd birthday. I was excited yet nervous. Mr. Wrong and my mom were waiting for me to walk out of the gate. It was a cloudy spring day in Troy Virginia, but I wouldn't have cared if it was raining.

We were in for a long ride, so my mom decided to stop by McDonald's for a quick bite to eat. I didn't order anything. I didn't have an appetite—I was in shell shock. I sat in the back seat with Mr. Wrong in silence as he talked in between bites about all the plans he had for us. How he would get us our own place (he was currently living with my mother, and so would I).

How he had already applied for better jobs making more money. He boasted about being proud to have been a changed man, leaving the streets alone and, finally, wanting to be legit. He even got my name tattooed on his arm. I felt like he was finally the man I had been praying for. And just maybe my life would finally get on track.

The first stop, once reaching Hampton Roads, was probation and parole. I wanted to handle my business first. It took a couple of hours. I met my probation officer, had a small conversation about my goals, got my assignments, and went about my day.

I didn't want to be out, especially in these clothes and no real shower, so we went on home. I got out of the car and walked inside, still feeling a bit anxious. I sat down and had a conversation with my mom. I took a shower but had to put on sweatpants because of the weight I gained. I had never been this big in my life.

I had gone from a size 2 to a size 18 jeans! It didn't look bad on me—or so I was told—because of my height. Big Bro and his wife took me shopping.

The kids were at school. My original release date was April 2nd, the day after my birthday, but with the jail credits being issued, it moved my date up. I asked my mom not to tell the kids as I wanted to surprise them.

Later that day, Mom went to pick up the kids. I waited in her room for them to arrive. Mr. Wrong had gone to work so I was able to just focus on them for the evening.

They walked in the house in their normal routine. Mom walked ahead of them in hopes that they would follow. They were used to dropping book bags, washing hands, and grabbing some kind of snack before anything else. Plus, Mom always needed at least 15 minutes of "wind down, alone time" after work.

She got about halfway up the hall and called them to follow. I wish I still had the video of their reaction. They walked in with the most confused look ever, stood there for a second, and the two oldest yelled out, "Mommy!" at the same time.

All three ran to my arms. Baby girl burst out in tears of joy, and so did I. Tears and laughter.

Mom cooked dinner for us all, I relaxed and snuggled up with my babies and listened to them tell me some of the things I missed. I put baby girl in the bath and all of them to bed. Mr. Wrong and I got a hotel for the night.

The next morning, we got up and went back to my mom's to get the kids ready for school. My first order of business was to put in that application. I put in the app, had a small interview with the manager, and was told to report the next day. I walked across the street to Walmart for pants and slip-resistant shoes, eager to start.

I worked at the same place as Mr. Wrong. I had served before for three and a half years, so I was overconfident that once I learned the menu, I would do well. And I did. We didn't have a car so we would usually walk or catch a ride from friends. Mostly Doll Face and Hell Raiser.

The kids seemed to be happier that I was home. Listening to them laugh and seeing their smiles brought so much joy to my heart. I stayed in and enjoyed the kids for about a week before linking up with friends.

Bestie had, of course, held me down during my bid but had reconnected with an old friend while I was away. They were hanging pretty tight and her and I were cool, so we instantly became three peas in a pod. We linked up and I wanted to smoke some weed so bad but couldn't because of probation. So, Mr. Wrong introduced me to spice.

It was a little different than the K2 I had used before. It gave a similar effect as weed, but once you got high, you were too high. Spaced out and nodding off like a heroin addict. At least that was the effect it gave me. I thought I could handle it, but I was so wrong. I became hooked. I continued to work but was quickly heading back down the wrong path.

I reconnected with some bad influences I would call friends at the time, who didn't try to persuade me to do better or the right things. By the end of summer, my world would come crashing down. I started to notice my oldest being distant and not her usual bubbly self. I tried to talk to her, and she tried to convince me she was ok.

My cousin came to town. Her and my oldest were close. She and I were more like sisters than cousins, so my oldest looked to her like an aunt. I'd had a previous conversation or two with my sister/cuz and she told me she would talk to her.

She came to town—we were invited to chill poolside with Bestie and her boo, so I went to get dressed so they could have some privacy. They talked, then we left to party.

On the ride to Bestie's location, my sister/cuz asked me a couple of hypothetical questions. I was extremely passionate about my responses, which would be the only reason I can think that she would leave it alone.

We arrived and began to turn up. We were waiting for Bestie to get dressed so we could go out to a local club. We got a little too wasted, it got later and later, so we stayed in. Sister/cuz, Bestie, and I were in conversation when the liquid courage quickly intruded into the conversation.

Sister/cuz started to ask questions and make statements that I felt were inappropriate to be discussing in front of Bestie's boo, so I asked her to change the subject.

She continued and said some rude things. I got upset and stood up. She stood up too.

The next thing I know, we were eye to eye, toe to toe. Ready to scrap. I wasn't going to disrespect, so I headed for the door.

Bestie and her boo were trying to calm us down. She pushed me but I held my composure. All I could think of was the month's prior conversation with my probation officer and all the time I still had over my head. So, I didn't hit her back at all. I just yelled and called her every name but a child of God.

She got more upset as Bestie's boo began to pull her to the car. She yelled to me, and I can still hear the words in my mind, loud and clear. She told me something that crushed my spirit. It was the ultimate betrayal that one could think of, involving my husband and another someone else that meant more to me than him.

I was crushed.

Bestie's boo ended up taking sister/cuz back to her car. He was extremely intoxicated, so he escorted me to the guest room for the night. I couldn't sleep. I kept calling Mr. Wrong, who was also out with friends (so he says). He didn't answer.

I began to fall asleep as soon as the birds started chirping. I slept for about three hours and then woke up to the smells of breakfast, swollen eyes, and a massive headache.

I got myself together in the guest bathroom and went downstairs. Bestie's boo had made us breakfast. I didn't have much of an appetite after receiving the news I got. So, I just drank some orange juice, ready to go home to confront Mr. Wrong.

Bestie's boo dropped me off. I took a long, hot shower, got dressed, and between tears, began to pack Mr. Wrong's belongings. He came home to everything he owned in a box to the left.

I was so upset; I couldn't even explain to him the reason why. But he knew. All his dark had come to the light. I didn't want an explanation because I knew it would be all lies. Once I calmed down, I gave him the benefit of the doubt and listened anyway. I asked question after question, over and over like Inspector Gadget. He couldn't keep up with his lies. He was no longer welcome in my mother's home. And although he betrayed me in the worst way, he still had a hold on me.

He would invite me to where he was to smoke spice and try to have sex. I couldn't stomach what he had done and was fighting with my flesh and gave in a couple of times. I could not make myself stop loving him. He had hurt me a million times before, but this pain cut deeper than I could imagine.

My mind hated him for all the lies, beating, and cheating, but my heart still wanted him because I was sick too. My grandma used to call it a soul tie. This one with him was double tied with about three small knots on the end.

I started to gain some of my power back with the love of my mama, my friends, and therapy. I was no longer in communication with Mr. Wrong. But I had spiraled all the way out of control with my habit.

I had started to lose the prison weight I gained, and when the pounds started shedding, so did my confidence. I was on a repeat cycle. My mom did her best to help me... even told my PO I was using spice.

The drug was so new, there was no test for it. He would have me provide a pee sample every visit and I would pass with flying colors. By then, I was only reporting bimonthly as I was still working and complying. By the time March 2015 came around, I was released from probation early after only being home for one year.

I worked at the restaurant until about April of 2015. I eventually went back to hotels. I was given my old position back at a hotel I previously worked at before prison. I was so thankful for the opportunity. I didn't give myself the chance to heal from the breakup of Mr. Wrong. I had caught the eye of another guy in Sept of 2014 at a wedding. We instantly clicked. Looking back, he was just a rebound.

He would become the one who would take and pick me up from work daily. In Jan of 2015, there was a bad snowstorm in our area. I was working multiple positions at the hotel. One of the housemen was snowed in, so I was asked to stay at the hotel and help make sure things ran smoothly. My new guy and I stayed at the hotel for three days straight. We got to know each other and were becoming closer.

His homeboy had recently come home from prison and was cutting my son's hair. He and I were cool too.

One day, he called me while My New Guy was out of town to tell me to focus on myself and that my new guy was not as cool as I thought. I wanted what I wanted, so I just pushed what he told me to the back of my head. I didn't mention it to My New Guy. I wanted him to see me as a "good girl" who "trusted" him.

About a week later, he called me up, furious.

He was questioning me about the conversation between his home boy and me. I told him what was told to me, and guess what? He ain't trust me!

He said I should have told him and that I wasn't to be trusted. As fast as it had started, it quickly came to an end. He continued to take me to work for a while. I got my own car about a month later and we remained friends, but I had broken his trust.

Honestly, I wasn't ready anyway.

I was still on the spice. It had gotten so bad that I was pawning jewelry and stealing Mama's change just to get it. I knew I had reached rock bottom when, one day, I left my pack in my bathrobe. She found it and had it on her person.

She told me not to bring it back in her house. I tried to fight her to get it back. I didn't win, of course. So, I just went and got some more.

The brand I smoked was popular. I wasn't the one to try all the varieties, but because Mama had stolen my pack, I had to improvise.

I tried a different brand. The next day, Mama came home with the kids to see me nodded out on the front porch like a real-life dope fiend. She took a picture for proof.

I finally left the spice alone and went back to weed.

I was also working for another hotel at this point too. That didn't last either.

Then I started working for a private cleaning company, and I had also connected with an old friend. One day, against my better judgment, I met up with him to have an itch scratched. It was just supposed to be that. We were friends, so he knew what I had been through. He was very supportive and wanted to help get me to a better situation. He had a three-bedroom house that only he was living in. He asked if he could help by moving us in. I thought it wouldn't be a bad idea. We would have our own space and my youngest two would have their own rooms. My oldest wanted to stay with my mom. So, I said, "Screw it!" and moved me and the kids in. We went from "friends" to being "booed up" in no time.

My old friend liked to party. I'm not sure why I thought things would be different once we had a title. He would come home in the wee hours of the morning—if he came home at all. It was always a dumb excuse that I had heard a million times before from Mr. Wrong, so I knew it was bullshit.

This eventually led to arguments until it became physical. He wouldn't beat my ass for no reason, but if I questioned him and it turned into an argument, it would almost always end in violence.

I had moved out and back in so many times, it was pathetic.

It wasn't all bad though.

He was actually the one who encouraged me to start my own cleaning company after hearing how I would so often take the lead on my current job.

So, in April of 2016, I started my own business. It was supposed to be with a friend, but we had a fall out, so I decided to do it on my own.

Things didn't work out between my old friend and me. I ended up moving back in with my mother. He was one of the ones that Ishould have definitely left in the friend zone. He was an awesome friend but when we crossed that line, I saw another side. The lies, cheating, and playing me against his ex (while occasionally cheating with her) became really old, real fast. Moving back home ended up being the better decision.

I started my business while still living with this old friend. I was hungry and determined for success.

I was so mad at myself for what felt like at the time throwing my life down the drain. For all my past, things I caused, ignored, and the things I didn't, I was just angry.

I got serious with advertising, expanding, and growing my business.

One day, I received a phone call from a property manager with the city of Hampton. They were inquiring about my cleaning services and wanted me to place a bid for an apartment complex. Three companies were asked to clean three units as our bid numbers were extremely close. I cleaned with compassion and detail and won the bid. Next thing I know, I was cleaning additional apartment complexes and different commercial buildings for the city.

I was on my way.

In March of 2017, I got a random call from a guy I had only encountered via social media and one previous phone call. He was interested in cleaning services. We had been Facebook friends for about two years.

I wasn't sure whether to take him seriously as he had played with my time with his first inquiry. My friends and I were about to take our kids on spring break vacation, and I could use the extra money, so I said, "Yes, ok."

I went to his apartment and did the move-out clean. He was attractive but not my usual type, so when he came in to check on me and flirt, I paid him no mind.

We exchanged some small talk about business and what plans I had for the weekend. I told him about the trip and that my birthday was the next day. He offered me a shot of vodka. I thought he was cool, and the gesture was nice.

The next day, he sent a Happy Birthday message, thanked me again, and admitted to having a "crush" on me. He then asked if we could meet up when we both came back in town. I said yes!

Our first date was at a popular bar in Hampton Virginia's Peninsula Town Center Mall.

We had dinner and drinks.

I liked that conversation with him because it was easy. It was as if we were old friends. His humor made me like him more. For the next couple of weeks, he and I would talk constantly, and we spent a lot of time together on the weekends.

One day, I wore an outfit that he wasn't too fond of. We met at a club. I had Bestie and the two other peas to our pod with me and he brought a friend to tag along with him. I wanted to impress him. Epic fail.

He made a comment about me not wearing it again. I looked at him like he was crazy because, for one, you don't buy my clothes, and for two, you ain't my man." Later that night, he made me his "girl."

I appreciated him for liking me for me. He was extremely interested in helping me better my business and myself. He admired my ambition and hard work, and I admired his knowledge and appreciated that he was simply intrigued with whatever came out of my mouth. We bounced off each other and made a great team.

In 2017, I got the keys to my brand-new place for me and my babies to start over. It was small and we didn't have any central heat or AC, but it was ours.

We were not too far from my mother and the kids loved that she was within walking distance. They have a close bond with my mother as she was the one who took care of them when I was away. I liked it too, especially on the days I didn't feel like cooking.

My new bae, whom we will call "the love of my life" didn't judge or look down on me for my living situation or the fact I was still trying to put my life back together. He was patient and understanding.

He would pull up to my little trailer in his 2017 Charger and not look down on me for not having the material things he had. He genuinely fell in love with my soul. So much that, not long after that, he moved me and my children out of the trailer into a luxury apartment.

He was patient and understanding. I was not completely healed. He helped me to love me past that pain and showed me I was worthy. I was enough.

I knew I was enough for myself, but I was scarred and scared to let another man get close to me or my children or to love again. He constantly showed me he was safe, and I could trust him.

So, we didn't stay in the apartment long. Not even a year. He said it made more sense to own.

In June of 2018, we purchased a home together. And then, on Thanksgiving of 2020 at our home, he surprised me and proposed.

Our wedding was Aug 13, 2022. The happiest day of my life!

I felt like all the hard work, all the tears, the addictions, the low self-esteem, and the rage in motion was not in vain.

About 30 or so days before my wedding, while scrolling through Facebook… I ran across "Mr. Wrong" on the 'People you may know' list. I had seen him in passing while working around the city and wondered why I didn't have any negative feelings when I saw him. Honestly, I just laughed. I had also seen him on the 'People you may know' list in the past and would immediately block the page. But this time, Spirit whispered, "You're ready." So, I sent this message:

"On normal occasions I would ask a person I haven't spoken to in a while how they are doing… I honestly pray you're ok and have gotten the help you need! I did!! I just want you to know that I don't hate you. I hate what you did and the outcome it created. But the outcome just so happened to be a highlight in my story. U DIDN'T BREAK ME!! There was a time when I would stop breathing for you… you took advantage of my love and my heart. I won't elaborate on that too much because I'm sure you know that already. I do need you to know that I thank you though! All of what you did to me was not in vain. What you tried to do to my daughter was not in vain. We are both doing extremely well! She's on her own with a car, apartment, and career. No babies either! I am getting married to the love of my life in 52 days. This is the last part of my healing process. I don't need you to respond. Just know Karma will have her day… if she already hasn't, and I swear I DON'T wish any ill harm or bad intentions on you because the moment I started forgiving you is the moment my blessings started pouring in! You don't have to ever admit what you did to my daughter or what you tried to do. You don't even have to apologize!! I won't block my blessing hating you… And I won't hold my breath waiting! You, my daughter, myself, and God know the truth. And it takes too much energy to hate you or wish bad on you in any way. Again, I pray you find your way and be a productive person, give something back to the community other than trauma, lies, and deceit. I pray God has mercy on your soul. I forgive you, sir!! My businesses are thriving. I'm happily in love, and my children, ALL of them, are fine! Peace and blessings to you and yours!"

And that was all the closure I needed!

I chose to take my power back.

I chose to forgive myself.

I chose to forgive all that wronged me.

I chose to forgive Mr. Wrong.

I chose to change my thinking.

I chose to become.

CONCLUSION

"Nature is so powerful, so strong. Capturing its essence is not easy—your work becomes a dance with light and the weather. It takes you to a place within yourself."
— Annie Leibovitz

"Keep walking through the storm. Your rainbow is waiting on the other side."
— Heather Stillufsen

No one has arrived!

Not even me.

The purpose of writing this book is for all the girls out there like me who grew up without the guidance of a father and looked for love in all the wrong places, instead of looking within! Also, for the girls who made a mistake or two and feel like they threw their whole lives away.

I haven't "arrived". Once we get over one thing, something else is bound to happen to make us have to heal again.

I still struggle with self-doubt, insecurities, and depression to this day, but I continue to watch my thinking, surround myself with positive people, and just keep swimming.

I surround myself with like-minded individuals (shout out to Eta Eta Lambda Society, Hampton, Virginia) who inspire and motivate me.

I've learned how to deal with this thing called life in a healthy way. I've learned we will continue to learn until the day we die, but only if we desire to.

Seasons come and seasons go, but one thing remains the same, and that is remembering what matters most.

It's all about how you move through the seasons!

Don't forget your umbrella and boots when it rains.

Have supplies stocked for hurricane season.

Prepare for "fall" harvest.

Rest, "hibernate", during the winter.

Reflect on what you learned in the spring and put what you learned into action in the summer.

We all have seasons of our lives.

Learning the lessons is what matters most.

Peace and blessings.

Love and light!